BIBLICAL EXEGESIS HANDBOOK

SECOND EDITION

Biblical Exegesis Handbook

Second Edition

Timothy P. Palmer

AFRICA CHRISTIAN TEXTBOOKS

2013

Biblical Exegesis Handbook
Second Edition
© 2013 Timothy Palmer

Africa Christian Textbooks (ACTS)

ACTS Bookshop, International HQ, TCNN,
PMB 2020, Bukuru, Plateau State, 930008, Nigeria
GSM: +234 (0) 803-589-5328; E-mail: pa@actsnigeria.org
Website: http://actsnigeria.org

ISBN: 9789789051885 Print
ISBN: 9789789053629 ePub
ISBN: 9789789053636 Mobi

Cover Design: Benjamin A. Bredeweg
Photo Credit: © Can Stock Photo Inc. / jgroup

CONTENTS

PREFACE

Biblical exegesis is the interpretation of a biblical text. What does a text in the Bible mean? Biblical exegesis attempts to discover the meaning of biblical texts.

Every theological student and pastor does exegesis. Some do exegesis well; others do it poorly. Often our preaching is poor because there has not been good exegesis.

A standard theological library will have textbooks on exegesis. But most of these textbooks are technical and difficult. Many of these textbooks are also written in the European or American context. It is clear that a simpler and contextual textbook on exegesis is needed.

This book proceeds out of more than 25 years of teaching at the Theological College of Northern Nigeria (TCNN). In these years I have supervised many exegetical theses and I have examined exegetical master's theses in vivas. I have also listened to many Nigerian sermons, some of which have been very powerful and others which have been very poor. Good exegesis is vital for the church.

Much of this book is technical. But after the technical part, teachers will want to assign practical exegetical essays to put the theory into practice. They should assign exegetical essays on Bible passages to practice the exegetical theory.

It is my prayer that this book will be useful to theological students and pastors as they seek to do exegesis in order to hear and apply Scripture in the African context.

Theological College of Northern Nigeria
Bukuru

PART I

WHAT IS EXEGESIS?

In our culture we have many texts. Communication often takes place through written texts.

The daily newspaper has a variety of texts. There are news reports, editorials, advertisements, obituaries and poems in the newspaper. Printed books also contain different types of texts: historical texts, scientific texts, fictional novels and religious devotionals. Personal or official letters are another type of text. We write letters applying for jobs or admission into a college; we also write personal letters to friends and prospective spouses. Legal documents are also texts. Today on our phones we have a relatively new way of communicating—texting. Young people often send short cryptic messages on their cell phones to friends. We call these messages text messages.

All texts have an author; most texts have a receiver or an audience; all texts are written in a cultural and historical environment; and every text has a meaning.[1] *Exegesis* is the process of interpreting the meaning of a text.

Everyone who reads a text exegetes the text. Usually the meaning of a text is clear. Then we intuitively exegete the text and understand

---

[1]See J. Hayes and C. Holladay, *Biblical Exegesis* (Louisville: Westminster John Knox, 2007), pp. 21-28.

the meaning. But sometimes the meaning of a text may not be immediately clear. For example: "Super Eagles defeat Gambia." (Is this a military victory?) Or: "Yankees beat Boston." (Who are the Yankees?) Or: "c u soon." (What language is this?)

In these cases, you may need to know the author of the text, the historical and cultural circumstances of the text and the nature of the text's language.

It is our assumption that a text has a single meaning. The writer of the sports report, the personal letter, the legal document and the text message writes a text with a single intended meaning. Exegesis is the process of understanding the single meaning of a text.

The Bible has many types of texts. There are legal documents, historical narratives, poetry, prophecy and the like. A serious student of the Bible needs to interpret these texts to discover their meaning.

Biblical exegesis is "the careful systematic study of the Scripture to discover the original, intended meaning."[2]

The Interpreter

Every text will usually have one or more readers or interpreters. The interpreter is the one who exegetes or interprets the text.

If you read the Bible privately or professionally, you are the exegete and interpreter. What kind of interpreter should you be?

On the one hand, interpretation is a scientific or technical exercise. The interpreter should use the techniques described in this book to come to an objective understanding of the text. The interpreter should be fair and objective in his or her interpretation. He or she should strive for objectivity in interpretation.

---

[2]G. Fee and D. Stuart, *How To Read the Bible for All Its Worth* (Jos: Potters House, 1999), p. 21.

But recent scholarship has reminded us that we all have presuppositions or prejudices. What type of presuppositions should you have in interpretation?

If, for example, the interpreter of Scripture is an unbeliever or an atheist, he or she may not be able to understand the true message of a passage. Such a person's presuppositions may not allow him or her to grasp the real possibility of one of Jesus' miracles.

The prejudices of an atheist might prevent such a person from really understanding many of the spiritual realities of Scripture.

Therefore, faith is an essential presupposition for understanding the Bible. "Only the one who believes and trusts in God can truly understand what God has spoken in his Word."[3] A biblical or Christian faith allows one to hear God's Word more clearly.

A Lutheran lecturer in Nigeria once gave this a more christological focus. Jonathan Preus said: "the 'Christ-principle' of Scriptural interpretation will be a fruitful prejudice, because it shines upon Scripture the very 'light of the world.'"[4]

A Christian or christological pre-understanding is important in understanding the text. But one must not let one's pre-understanding prevent a true understanding of the text. One must avoid pure subjectivity in doing exegesis.

Exegesis is a rigorous discipline that strives to discover the original meaning of a text. There is thus a careful balance between objectivity and subjectivity in the interpretation of Scripture.

---

[3]W. Klein et al., *Introduction to Biblical Interpretation* (Nashville: Thomas Nelson, 2004), p. 136.

[4]J. Preus, *Reading the Bible through Christ* (Bukuru: Africa Christian Textbooks, 1997), p. 132.

Meaning of a Text

The goal of exegesis is to discover the meaning of a text. This is true both in our contemporary world and in the world of the Bible.

The sports report, the personal letter, the text message and the car advertisement each has a single meaning. The sports report describes a football match; the personal letter expresses one's feelings; the text message has a brief message; the car advertisement describes the virtues of a car.

In the same way, every text in Scripture has a single meaning. This is the meaning intended by the author. The goal of exegesis is to discover the meaning intended by the author.

To use the words of some scholars: "The aim of good interpretation is simple: to get at the 'plain meaning of the text.'"[5] And, "the author-encoded historical meaning of these texts remains the central objective of hermeneutics."[6]

This has not always been the understanding of the church. The early church was troubled by the physical nature of the Old Testament and sometimes claimed that a text had two meanings—a literal and spiritual meaning. The medieval western church eventually claimed that a text has four meanings—a literal, allegorical, moral and eschatological meaning.[7]

The fourfold meaning of a text satisfied some pastoral and theological concerns. But the result was exegetical confusion. Which meaning is the real meaning of a text? Who determines the meaning of a text? Where is God's Word to the reader?

The Reformation called for an end to this confusion. Martin Luther wrote:

---

[5] Fee and Stuart, *How To Read the Bible for All Its Worth*, p. 16.
[6] W. Klein et al., *Introduction to Biblical Hermeneutics*, p. 185.
[7] See J. Preus, *Reading the Bible through Christ*, p. 42.

> The Holy Spirit is the simplest writer and adviser in heaven
> and on earth. That is why his words could have no more than
> the one simplest meaning which we call the written one, or the
> literal meaning of the tongue.[8]

Luther argued that an exegete should search for the "literal meaning"
or the "grammatical, historical meaning."[9]

The Protestant Reformation thus launched the *grammatico-historical method* of interpreting Scripture. John Bright defines this method:

> The text is to be taken as meaning what its words most
> plainly mean in light of the situation (historical situation or
> life situation) to which they were originally addressed: the
> "grammar" is to be interpreted against the background of
> "history."[10]

The grammatico-historical method then determines the exegetical method. Bright continues:

> It becomes, therefore, the task of the student to determine as
> accurately as he can . . . what [the author] *actually intended to
> say.* In this way alone can the true meaning of the biblical word
> be arrived at; and it is the biblical word in its true meaning, and
> that alone, that can claim to be normative in the church.[11]

This, Bright says, is

> the task of *exegesis*—of reading from the biblical text the
> meaning its author intended to convey. We are not permitted
> the luxury of *eisegesis*—of reading our own ideas into the text

---

[8] M. Luther, "Answer to . . . Emser," in *Luther's Works* 39:178.

[9] M. Luther, "Answer to . . . Emser," in *Luther's Works* 39:181.

[10] J. Bright, *The Authority of the Old Testament* (Nashville: Abingdon, 1967), p. 42.

[11] J. Bright, *The Authority of the Old Testament*, p. 42.

or finding there meanings which its author did not have in mind.[12]

This has been the dominant exegetical method of the last 500 years. The assumption was that each text has one single meaning and that the grammatico-historical method is the proper way for understanding this single meaning. This is the **modern** understanding of exegesis.

The modern view of exegesis assumes that a text has one meaning but many applications. The text's one meaning can be applied in different contexts.

For example, Leviticus 19:33 says: "When an alien lives with you in your land, do not mistreat him."[13] The meaning of this text is clear: the Israelites in the Old Testament times should be kind to the aliens in their land. This is the single *meaning* of the text.

But the *application* of the text might differ from culture to culture. The peculiar situation of aliens in Zimbabwe and South Africa might differ from the situation of aliens in Nigeria. The text then might be applied differently in each separate culture.

Similarly, the *meaning* of Jesus' words in John's Gospel are clear: "This is my command: love each other" (Jn 15:17). But the *application* of these words will vary from situation to situation.

The following diagram illustrates the modern view of exegesis, where A1, A2 and A3 refer to three different applications of the meaning of a text.

---

[12]J. Bright, *The Authority of the Old Testament*, pp. 42-43; italics added.

[13]Scripture quotations are from the New International Version (NIV). Sometimes the NIV translation is modified to reflect better the original sense.

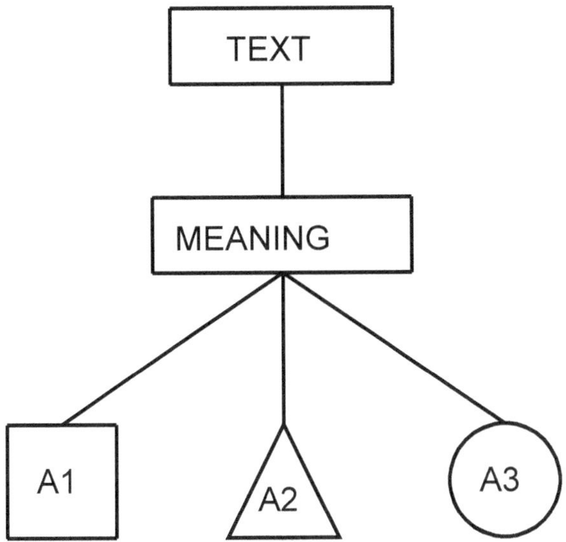

In this diagram, exegesis will attempt to explain the original or intended meaning of the author. Once the original meaning is understood, then the text needs to be applied to our respective situations and cultures.

But in the last few decades the modern view has been challenged by **postmodernism**. Postmodernism thinks that a text does not have a single meaning determined by the author. Instead, a single text will have as many meanings as there are readers.

In the modern view of exegesis, the meaning of the text is determined by the author. In the postmodern view of exegesis, the meaning of a text is determined by the reader. But then a text will have many meanings instead of one.

The following diagram illustrates the postmodern view of exegesis, where M1, M2 and M3 refer to three different meanings of a text.

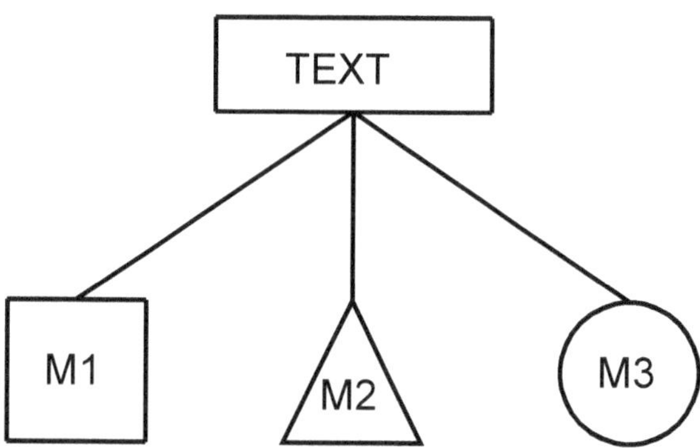

This diagram shows that postmodernism blurs the distinction between meaning and application. Meaning and application are the same for postmodernism.

But the examples at the beginning of this chapter show that a text has one meaning. If a history book says that Nigeria became independent on October 1, 1960, this is a historical statement that has a single meaning. If a woman writes a letter applying for a job, her letter will have a single meaning. If an advertisement praises a certain type of vehicle, this means that the car is worth buying.

The problem with the postmodern view of exegesis is that it gives absolute subjectivity to the text. A text then loses its authoritative meaning. A text then can mean anything. If this is the case, the Word of God is no longer normative or authoritative.

One writer warned: "The subjectivity of modern exegesis must be brought under control, lest truth be forfeited."[14] It is essential for our faith and our life that we receive God's intended message in his Word.

This writer insists: "the author's intended meaning [is] the true core of biblical interpretation."[15] The goal of exegesis should be "the original meaning of a text" or "the intended meaning of a text."[16]

Yet, the text needs to be applied to our lives. A text will have one meaning but many applications. The text needs to be applied to our situation. Therefore, "our hermeneutical task is not finished until we as the contemporary audience have *applied* the meaning that we think the author is communicating."[17]

The Bible as the Word of God

The church has confessed that the Bible is not just a human document but also the Word of God. This belief is based on the New Testament view of the Old Testament. Paul in 2 Timothy 3:16 says that "all Scripture (*graphē*) is God-breathed." The Scripture that Paul was referring to was the Old Testament; but by the principle of extension

---

[14]G. Osborne, *The Hermeneutical Spiral* (Downers Grove: InterVarsity Press, 2006), p. 518.

[15]G. Osborne, *The Hermeneutical Spiral*, p. 466.

[16]G. Osborne, *The Hermeneutical Spiral*, p. 520.

[17]W. Kaiser in *Introduction to Biblical Hermeneutics* (Grand Rapids: Zondervan, 2007), p. 322.

or extrapolation we assume that the New Testament is also God-breathed. Peter explains the process of inspiration: "prophecy never had its origin in the will of man, but men spoke from God as they were carried along by the Holy Spirit" (2 Pet. 1:21).

If Scripture is the Word of God, it will then be authoritative. John Bright says: "The final authority in all matters of faith and conduct is the Bible." And, "the God of the Bible is the Christian's supreme authority in all senses of the word."[18]

But, "if the Bible is to be normative in matters of faith and conduct, it must be the Bible rightly interpreted."[19] This is why exegesis is so important. Exegesis enables us to hear the Word of God.

Exegesis is also important for preaching. Bright says: "We shall never have strong preaching . . . until our pastors . . . consistently base their sermons in the authority of the Word."[20] Bright continues:

> There can, therefore, be no substitute for biblical preaching.
> Biblical preaching is the only kind that carries with it authority.
> And the preacher needs authority.[21]

If Scripture is God's Word to us, then we need to understand the words of Scripture properly. Exegesis is an essential tool for interpreting and understanding what God is trying to tell us in the Bible.

---

[18]J. Bright, *The Authority of the Old Testament*, pp. 23, 31.

[19]J. Bright, *The Authority of the Old Testament*, p. 41.

[20]J. Bright, *The Authority of the Old Testament*, p. 165.

[21]J. Bright, *The Authority of the Old Testament*, p. 166.

Study Questions

1. What is exegesis?
2. Should an interpreter of Scripture have presuppositions? Which presuppositions should he or she have?
3. Why is it dangerous for an interpreter to have presuppositions?
4. How many meanings will a Bible text have? How many applications will a Bible text have?
5. Why did the early church use the allegorical method of interpretation? Is such a method proper? Why or why not?
6. What is the grammatico-historical method of interpretation?
7. Evaluate the postmodern view of exegesis.
8. Why is proper exegesis important for the church?

PART II

DOING EXEGESIS

Exegesis is vital to the church. Exegesis is the process of understanding God's Word for us.

There are two basic parts to exegesis: *context* and *content*. An exegete will first want to consider the historical and literary context of the text; then the exegete will examine the content of the text.[22]

A thesis might want to devote one chapter to the context (historical and literary) and another chapter to the content. The application of a text will normally follow the strictly exegetical parts (See sample thesis outlines at the end of this book).

The ten steps below describe the main elements in the exegetical process. A student may select or arrange these steps as he or she sees fit. It is not necessary to follow the sequence below.

---

[22]See Fee and Stuart, *How To Read the Bible for All Its Worth*, p. 23.

CHAPTER 1

CHOOSE A PERICOPE

The first step in doing exegesis is to choose your text. The text should be "a genuine self-contained unit."[1] Sometimes this self-contained unit is called a *pericope*[2] (pronounce as: per-i-co-pe).

"An exegesis paper considers a passage that is a complete unit of manageable size."[3] The passage should not be too long or too short.

A paragraph division in an English translation of the Bible is often a good guide for an appropriate passage. It is also useful to consult the Hebrew or the Greek text. A pericope will have one or more complete sentences in the original language. It would be wrong to have only a fragment of a complete Hebrew or Greek sentence as part of your passage.

Sometimes the text will give indicators of the beginning or the end of a pericope. Prophetic oracles, for example, are often marked off by phrases like "Thus says Yahweh" or "says Yahweh." For example, Amos 1:2 is a self-contained unit introduced by "he said." Amos 1:3-5

---

[1] D. Stuart, *Old Testament Exegesis* (Louisville: Westminster John Knox, 2009), p. 5; G. Fee, *New Testament Exegesis* (Louisville: Westminster John Knox, 2002), p. 9.

[2] D. Stuart, *Old Testament Exegesis*, p. 5.

[3] M. Gorman, *Elements of Biblical Exegesis* (Peabody, Mass.: Hendrickson, 2009), p. 37.

is another pericope or oracle introduced by "This is what Yahweh says" and concluded by "says Yahweh."

A parable of Jesus would be a self-contained unit. It would wrong to do an exegetical study of only a part of the parable.

But sometimes in the case of a longer historical narrative or prophecy you will need to choose a smaller, more manageable text. In every case, we need to recognize that the pericope is part of a longer literary unit. Your exegesis will need to recognize the longer literary context of your pericope.

Chapter divisions in our Bibles are not always an infallible guide to separate exegetical units. The first verse of 1 Corinthians 11, for example, belongs to the literary unit at the end of chapter 10, and not to chapter 11.[4]

A manageable self-contained unit may vary from a few verses to 15 or 20 verses. A passage longer than 15 or 20 verses will probably be too long for an exegetical study.

The passage that you choose should be of interest and relevance to you or your ministry. All exegesis should be done in the interest of building the church of Jesus Christ.

---

[4]See M. Gorman, *Elements of Biblical Exegesis*, p. 38.

Study Questions

1. What is a pericope?
2. What are some guidelines for selecting a pericope?
3. Identify 7 pericopes in Amos 1.
4. Identify 7 pericopes in Luke 6.

CHAPTER 2

ESTABLISH AND PRINT THE TEXT

The focus of your exegesis will be the original Hebrew, Aramaic or Greek text of your passage. You should print this text at the beginning of your exegetical paper.

We have reasonable certainty as to the original wording of the biblical text. Generally the text in the Hebrew Bible or the Greek New Testament is an accurate reflection of the original text.

If there are no obvious problems in the Hebrew or Greek text, you can simply copy and paste the words of the Hebrew or Greek Bibles into your thesis. You should then footnote the source of your Hebrew or Greek text.

If you simply copy and paste an accepted text, you may skip the following section.

But in doing exegesis we must recognize that we do not have the original manuscripts of the biblical authors. We do not have the original manuscript of Isaiah or Mark or Paul. (These original manuscripts are called *autographs*.)

Instead, the original manuscripts of the biblical authors have been copied, and these copies have been copied again, and so the process continued for hundreds of years. The result is thousands of manuscripts of the Bible or parts of the Bible. In the process of copying, scribes sometimes made minor changes. What then was the original text or autograph of the author?

Usually the manuscripts agree on the wording of a text. Where there is widespread agreement, we know what the biblical author wrote. Usually there is little doubt about what the biblical author wrote.

But sometimes there are small differences among the manuscripts. For example, in Colossians 1:7, some manuscripts have "our behalf" while others have "your behalf." These two options are called *textual variants* or *variant readings*.

So what did Paul write? What was the original text in this place? To answer this question, we need to study the manuscripts. The most important manuscripts are mentioned at the bottom of our Hebrew or Greek Bibles.

Textual criticism is the attempt to find out what the original text said. Textual criticism "attempts to reconstruct the original text" of Scripture.[1] Textual criticism studies the evidence of the manuscripts to determine what the autograph said.[2] Textual criticism studies the manuscripts to determine the original words of Isaiah or Mark or Paul.

In order to do textual criticism, we have to know which manuscripts are stronger and which are weaker.

For the Old Testament, the most important manuscripts are the Hebrew Masoretic texts. The Masoretes were Hebrew scholars in the early Middle Ages who copied the Hebrew text but also added vowels. The Masoretic Hebrew text is usually the strongest text.

But there are other important versions of the Old Testament to consider. The Septuagint is the ancient Greek translation of the Old

---

[1] W. Egger, *How To Read the New Testament* (Peabody, Mass.: Hendrickson, 1996), p. 37.

[2] See *Hayes and Holladay*, Biblical Exegesis, p. 37.

Testament. The Qumran or Dead Sea Scrolls (**Q**) contains parts of the Hebrew Old Testament. The Syriac translation of the Old Testament is called Peshitta (**P**). The Aramaic translation of the Old Testament is called the Targum (**T**). Finally, Jerome's Latin translation of the Old Testament is called the Vulgate (**V**). These and other versions are listed at the beginning of the Biblia Hebraica. The versions are represented by the capital letters above which we put in parentheses.[3]

When there are textual variants, the student should decide which textual variant to adopt. He or she will have to evaluate both the quality of the manuscripts and the content of the variants.

For example, the Hebrew Masoretic text of 1 Samuel 8:16 says that the king will take "your menservants and maidservants and the best of your young men and donkeys."

But the footnote in the Hebrew Bible tells you that the Greek Septuagint has "your cattle and donkeys" instead of "your young men and donkeys." So which would be the original text? In this case, the sense of the Septuagint better fits Hebrew parallelism and probably reflects the original text.[4]

The notes in the Hebrew Bible are very difficult to understand. There are books that explain the system of notation.[5] Otherwise, the student should rely on footnotes in the English Bible and the comments of commentaries.

For the New Testament we have more than 5000 manuscripts or manuscript fragments of the Greek New Testament.[6] Again

---

[3]See D. Stuart, *Old Testament Exegesis*, pp. 88-89; E. Brotzman, *Old Testament Textual Criticism* (Grand Rapids: Baker, 1994), pp. 104-5.

[4]This example is from D. Stuart, *Old Testament Exegesis*, pp.37-38.

[5]A good source is E. Brotzman, *Old Testament Textual Criticism* (Grand Rapids: Baker, 1994).

[6]For this discussion, see K. Aland and B. Aland, *The Text of the New Testament* (Grand Rapids: Eerdmans, 1989).

the student needs to evaluate the manuscripts. Generally the older manuscripts are more reliable. Your Greek New Testament should list these manuscripts and give the dates.

Most of the oldest manuscripts are papyri, written on sheets of papyrus. They are indicated with the letter **p**. The manuscripts **p32**, **p46**, **p64**, **p66** and **p67** are some of the earliest manuscripts, dating from around AD 200. (**p52** and **p90** are even older than AD 200.)

All of the manuscripts before the Emperor Constantine are extremely valuable because of their age. (Constantine became a Christian in AD 312.) They were all written before Christianity became a state religion. But most of these manuscripts are only fragments of the New Testament.

After AD 300, we have codices (book manuscripts) written in the uncial (rounded) script containing all or much of the Bible. Codex Sinaiticus, found in a monastery on Mount Sinai, is particularly important. It dates from AD 325, and is known by the symbol ℵ (or, 01). Codex Vaticanus is from the same time, and is known by the letter **B** (or, 03). Codex Bezae (**D**, or, 05), from the fifth century, is also important.

There is general agreement among the manuscripts for most of the text of the New Testament. But sometimes there will be textual variants. English Bibles may have footnotes to a different reading of "some manuscripts." The footnotes or critical apparatus of the Greek New Testament will show the main textual variants.

For example, in Colossians 1:7, the textual variant "our" has strong support, including that of **p46**. The manuscripts supporting "your" are later and not as strong. Therefore, we assume that Paul wrote "on our behalf" and not "on your behalf."

Another example is Ephesians 1:1. Some manuscripts read: "to the saints in Ephesus, the faithful in Christ Jesus." Others read: "to the saints, the faithful in Christ Jesus." So did Paul write "in Ephesus" or not?

The critical apparatus of the Greek Bible shows strong support for "in Ephesus." But **p46** and a few other manuscripts omit "in Ephesus." The student must decide whether he thinks that Paul wrote these words or not.

A big question is the longer ending of the Gospel of Mark. Did Mark end his Gospel with verse 8 or with verse 20? The NIV, after verse 8, says: "The two most reliable early manuscripts do not have Mark 16:9-20." If you check your Greek New Testament, you will discover that Codex Sinaiticus (‭א‬) and Codex Vaticanus (**B**) do not have the longer ending. These two manuscripts end the Gospel of Mark with verse 8.

External criteria (the quality of the manuscripts, which in this case are very old) suggest that Mark ended his Gospel in verse 8. But what of the internal criteria or the theology of these verses? Is it likely that Mark ended his Gospel with the words "for they were afraid"? It is possible. One should study the biblical concept of fear. But does this fear refer to amazement or fear in the face of the resurrection of Jesus?

A few principles will help you decide what might be the original reading. There are both external and internal criteria.[7]

External criteria are the quality of the manuscripts. First, a particular variant is strong if it is found in many manuscripts. We call this *multiple attestation*. Second, the older manuscripts generally are stronger than the more recent ones. Third, a variant is strong if it is found in manuscripts from different geographic areas.

Internal criteria look at the variant itself. A few principles are suggested. First, the more difficult reading is likely to be the genuine reading. The reason is that scribes sometimes simplify difficult

---

[7]These criteria are taken from W. Egger, *How To Read the New Testament*, pp. 42-43.

readings as they copy. Second, a shorter reading is more likely to be genuine. Third, the reading that corresponds to the style of the author may be original. Fourth, if the reading is not influenced by parallel passages, it is likely to be genuine.

The goal of textual criticism is to establish what we think is the original text, the text that was inspired by the Holy Spirit. In the vast majority of the cases, there is little doubt about what the original writer wrote. One writer said that

> the overwhelming majority of variants are inconsequential, comprised mainly of spelling differences, the presence or absence of the article, changes in word order, and accidental omissions.[8]

When you have arrived at what you believe to be the original Hebrew or Greek text, you should produce this text in your thesis or paper. If necessary, explain any issue relating to variants.

---

[8]D. Deppe, *All Roads Lead to the Text* (Grand Rapids: Eerdmans, 2011), p. 39.

Study Questions

1. What is an autograph of a Bible text?
2. What is a textual variant or variant reading?
3. Why do we have textual variants or variant readings?
4. Name six important versions of the Old Testament text.
5. Do you think that Mark ended his Gospel with verse 8 or with verse 20? Why?
6. Why is the difficult variant likely to be the genuine variant?
7. What is the goal of textual criticism?

CHAPTER 3

PRODUCE AN ENGLISH TRANSLATION

After you produce the Hebrew or Greek text, you should produce an English translation. This translation could be your own translation or that of an existing Bible translation.

Today we have many Bible translations. Which translation is suitable for exegesis? Which types of translations do we have?

First of all, we must remember that no translation is a "perfect" one. A Bible translation is an attempt to bridge the cultural and linguistic gap between the ancient Hebrew or Jewish people and our contemporary culture. Thus, "every translation is itself an interpretation."[1]

There are two or three main categories of translations.[2]

At one end of the spectrum are *literal translations*, which are also called formal translations or formal-equivalence translations. These translations tend to be word-for-word renderings of the text. The King

---

[1] M. Gorman, *Elements of Biblical Exegesis*, p. 40.

[2] See Fee and Stuart, *How To Read the Bible for All Its Worth*, pp. 35-37; M. Gorman, *Elements of Biblical Exegesis*, pp. 41-44; W. Egger, *How To Read the New Testament*, pp. 56-59.

James Version (KJV), the New American Standard Bible (NASB) and the English Standard Version (ESV) are the most literal translations.

At the other end of the spectrum are *free translations* or functional-equivalence translations. Such translations attempt a thought-for-thought translation. Examples of free translations would be the Good News Bible (GNB) and the New Living Translation (NLT).

Both types of translations have advantages and drawbacks. But one exegete thinks that a literal translation is best for exegesis for two reasons:

> It allows more of the original ambiguities in the text to stand . . . ; and it generally renders a recurring key word in the original biblical text with the same English word in the translation.[3]

The problem with functional-equivalence or free translations is that they frequently "oversimplify complex or ambiguous texts and substitute contemporary idiom for ancient biblical idiom, often resulting in inconsistent or misleading translations of key items."[4] In other words, significant interpretations or exegetical choices are already being made in the translation.

Thus, the New Living Translation and the Good News Bible should *not* be used for serious exegesis. In the New Living Translation, "too many exegetical judgments were made"; likewise, the Good News Bible "should be viewed as one possible exegetical and stylistic rendering of the text. It should not be the sole basis for serious study."[5]

On the other hand, the King James Version (KJV) and the New King James Version (NKJV) should not be used because "they worked

---

[3]M. Gorman, *Elements of Biblical Exegesis*, p. 43.
[4]M. Gorman, *Elements of Biblical Exegesis*, pp. 43-44.
[5]M. Gorman, *Elements of Biblical Exegesis*, pp. 49, 50.

with generally late and less reliable biblical manuscripts."[6] The King James Version is based on the Textus Receptus of Erasmus, which used late manuscripts. Thus the King James translation does not always reflect the earlier and more reliable manuscripts.

Fee and Stuart see a spectrum of translations from the most literal to the most free. They think the ideal translation would be in between the two extremes. They call such a translation a dynamic-equivalence one. In 1982 they concluded: "the basic translation for reading and studying should be something like the NIV."[7]

The following diagram, which I have updated, illustrates this spectrum.[8]

Literal		**Dinamic Equivalence**	**Free**
KJV	RSV	NIV	GNB
NASB	NRSV	TNIV	NLT
ESV			

You should put the English translation of your text after the Hebrew or Greek text. You should give a footnote indicating whether the translation is yours or an existing Bible translation.

---

[6]M. Gorman, *Elements of Biblical Exegesis*, p. 51.
[7]Fee and Stuart, *How To Read the Bible for All Its Worth*, p. 36.
[8]Fee and Stuart, *How To Read the Bible for All Its Worth*, p. 36.

Study Questions

1. Why is there no "perfect" Bible translation?
2. What is a formal-equivalence and a function-equivalence translation?
3. Describe the strengths and weaknesses of a free translation.
4. Describe the strengths and weakness of a literal translation.
5. Why should the NLT, GNB and KJV not be used as a translation for exegesis?

CHAPTER 4

GIVE THE HISTORICAL CONTEXT

Every text has a historical context.

On September 5, 2012, Musa Ahmadu wrote the Bursar telling him that he had no money. The historical context of the text was the fact that his rice farm was destroyed in the floods of 2012.

On October 1, 2012, Emmanuel Chukwu wrote Ngozi expressing his affection for her. The historical context of the text was the fact that Emmanuel was still single at the age of 28 and that he wanted to marry Ngozi.

On October 14, 2012, *ThisDay* newspaper published a story on the Super Eagle victory over Liberia. The historical context of the text was the football game of October 13 when Nigeria beat Liberia 6-1.

All texts have a historical context. It is important, if possible, to know the historical context of a text to understand the text. Knowledge of the context of a text will help us to understand the text itself.

All Bible texts also have a historical context. It is important for an exegete to discover the historical context of a text in order to understand the text.

Two types of history are relevant here: the history of the text and the history *in* the text.[1]

The history *of* the text describes the circumstances in which the text was written. For example, on September 5, 2012, Musa wrote the Bursar because the Bursar was going to send him out of class. The text or letter was written in an academic setting on September 5. The history of the text is the circumstances in the College that caused Musa to write the letter.

But there is also a history *in* the text. The history in the text is the history of Musa's farm which was destroyed by the floods earlier in the rainy season. The history in the text is the history of the flooding.

In a similar way, 1 Kings 1-11 tells the story of King Solomon. The history *in* the text is the history of Solomon who reigned from about 970 to 930 BC. It is important to know the historical setting of King Solomon.

But the history of this text (1 Kings 1-11) is the writing of this text during the Babylonian captivity 400 years later (586 to 538 BC). (The end of Kings tells of the captivity of King Zedekiah who went into exile in 586 BC, so we assume that Kings was written after 586 BC.) During the exile someone wrote the final version of Kings in order to call God's people back to God.

In a similar way, the history *in* the book of Matthew is not the same as the history *of* the book of Matthew. The history *in* Matthew is the story of Jesus, who lived from about 4 BC to about AD 29. It is important to know the historical circumstances of Jesus: the Roman Empire and the life of the Jewish people in this Empire.

But what is the history *of* Matthew's Gospel? Matthew was probably written after the destruction of Jerusalem in AD 70 at a time when the church was being persecuted by unbelieving Jews and

---

[1]Hayes and Holladay, *Biblical Exegesis*, p. 53.

perhaps by the Romans. In this context, Matthew's Gospel was written to persuade the Jews that Jesus is the Messiah.

Of course, sometimes the history *of* the text and the history *in* the text are much the same. The book of Amos was probably written around 750 *BC* during the reign of King Jeroboam II. The historical circumstances of the book are the apostasy in the northern kingdom of Israel at that time.

Likewise, the history *of* the book of Philemon and the history *in* the book are almost identical. The apostle Paul wrote the book of Philemon during his ministry to persuade his friend Philemon to free the slave Onesimus.

We will now briefly consider these two types of history.

History of the text

The history of the text deals with the historical situation of the text. Who is the author? Who is the audience? What is the date? What is the historical situation that prompted the writing of the text?

Author and date

To understand a text, it would be useful to know who the author is and when he wrote the book. This would be a first step in understanding the historical background of the text.

If we know the author and the approximate date, we should state it clearly. If the author or date are unknown, we may be able to deduce the approximate time and setting of the text.

A common mistake in theological colleges and universities is to spend an inordinate amount of time discussing authorship or date. It is not necessary to write many pages discussing the obvious or something not directly relevant to your main thesis.

In the end, you will have to take a stand. Did Paul write the epistle of Titus or not? What would be the approximate date of Titus if Paul indeed wrote it?

Audience

If possible, it would be useful to know the audience of a Bible book. Was the audience of Kings the exiles in Babylon? Was the audience of Chronicles the returned exiles? Was the audience of Matthew early Christians facing persecution? Who was the audience of the book of Revelation?

Historical situation

In the end, we want to know as much as possible about the historical situation of the book. Where was the author when he was writing his book? What historical circumstances led him to write this book? Who was his audience?

If the audience of Kings is the people in exile, this will help us understand the theology and purpose of the book. Perhaps the author of Kings was calling the people back to God.

If the audience of Chronicles is the Jewish people back in Jerusalem, this will help us understand the book. Perhaps the author was trying to encourage God's people who returned.

If the audience of Matthew's Gospel is persecuted Christians, this might help us understand the relevance of some of Jesus' sayings.

If the audience of the book of Revelation was being persecuted by the Romans, this may help us to understand the significance of John's visions.

It is good to know as much as possible about the historical setting of a Bible book.

History in the text

Some books of the Bible tell history. The Torah tells the history of the patriarchs and the exodus and the sojourn in the wilderness. It would be useful to put these events in the larger historical setting. When did these people live and when did these events happen?

We should know the history of the people of Israel from the beginnings to the exile and the return from captivity. How does our historical narrative fit into the broader history?

We should also know the historical context of Jesus and the early church. How does our New Testament text fit into this history? How does this history fit into the broader history of the Jews and the Roman Empire?

Since every text has a historical context, it is important to know both the history of the text and the history in the text.

Study Questions

1. Distinguish between the history of a text and the history in the text.
2. What is the history in the text of 1 Kings 16:21-28? What is the history of this text?
3. What is the historical context of the book of Zephaniah?
4. What is the history in the text of Luke 2:1-7? What is the history of this text?
5. What is the historical context of the book of Philippians?

CHAPTER 5

DETERMINE THE GENRE

In our contemporary society there are many genres or types of literature. We have already considered a few examples.

A student writes a letter of apology to the Bursar. This is a letter of apology or petition. A young man writes a letter of affection to a young lady. This is a letter of affection.

A newspaper gives a report of a football game. A textbook may tell the history of a nation. These are both historical reports, but the language and style of the sports report will probably differ from that of the historical narrative.

There are legal documents or Certificates of Occupancy (C of Os) which describe a piece of property. There are also newspaper advertisements trying to sell this same piece of property. A legal document will differ from an advertisement in its style of writing.

Different genres contain different styles of writing. A historical narrative tends to be factual, although it will have its own presuppositions and purposes. The sports report may use hyperbole. ("Our team is obviously the best team in the world.") The letter of affection may use metaphors or similes in addition to hyperbole. ("You are as sweet as honey.") The C of O will use legal language.

The Bible also has many different types or genres of literature. An acquaintance of these genres will help us to understand texts. We now consider some of these genres.

Narrative

At least one-third of the Bible is narrative. Biblical narrative tells the history of God's people from the beginnings to the time of the early church. There is narrative in the Torah, the historical writings, the Gospels and Acts.

One needs to remember that this history is interpreted or theological history. It is history that is told to make a theological point. It is often sermonic in nature.

This is clear, for example, in the historical writings. In its final form, the history of Israel, from the entry into the Promised Land until the exile, was written to remind God's people of their covenantal responsibilities and of God's covenantal faithfulness.

One needs to listen carefully and sensitively to the message of a biblical narrative. Exegesis of narrative requires literary analysis. *Literary analysis* is

> the manifold varieties of minutely discriminating attention to the artful use of language, to the shifting play of ideas, conventions, tone, sound, imagery, syntax, narrative viewpoint, compositional units, and much else.[1]

Literary analysis will pay attention to key words in the story. It will listen to the actions and dialogue recorded. In so doing, it will try to determine what the narrator is trying to say.[2]

---

[1] R. Alter, *The Art of Biblical Narrative* (New York: Basic Books, 2011), p. 13.
[2] See R. Alter, *The Art of Biblical Narrative*, pp. 223-230.

For example, the reference to the barrenness of Michal (2 Sam 7:23) helps us understand the story of the bringing of the ark into Jerusalem. Nathan's words "You are the man!" (2 Sam 12:7) are decisive for understanding the story of David and Bathsheba. The words of the people at Mount Carmel, "Yahweh is God," (1 Kings 18:39) and the fire from heaven are critical for understanding this story.

A big danger in interpreting narratives is subjectivism or eisegesis. In other words, it is too easy to read our own theology or morality into a biblical story.

For example, preachers have used the story of the Tower of Babel to teach the positive principle of cooperation in building and other efforts. But this is not the teaching of Genesis 11. A careful reading of this text shows that those who work together against God will be frustrated.

Again, the Joseph story in Genesis has been plundered by well-meaning preachers for ethical applications. In so doing, the floodgate of subjectivism is swung wide open. Instead,

> the narrative is telling you what God did with an unlikely candidate for success. It does not contain any rules for getting ahead in business or life in general.[3]

Interpretation of Old Testament narratives should focus especially on what God is doing in a story. After all, the Bible is the story of God's redemptive acts in history.

Legal literature

The Torah has many laws and much legal material. They occur in different forms.[4]

---

[3] See Fee and Stuart, *How To Read the Bible for All Its Worth*, p. 79.
[4] See W. Klein et al., *Introduction to Biblical Interpretation*, pp. 341-44.

Casuistic laws (or case laws) have an "if . . . then . . ." format. The "if" clause describes the offence; the "then" clause states the penalty. The first part of Exodus 22 has some casuistic laws. They are specific laws relating to Israel's life in the Promised Land.

Apodictic laws are absolute commands or laws not having a conditional clause. The Ten Commandments in Exodus 20 and Deuteronomy 5 are examples of apodictic laws.

It should be noted that the laws in the Torah are embedded either in a historical narrative or a sermonic context. The laws of Exodus, Leviticus and Numbers are embedded in the historical journey of the Israelite people from Egypt to the Promised Land. The laws of Deuteronomy are embedded in Moses' sermon to the people before they enter the Promised Land.

It is also significant to note that Israel's laws were given in a covenantal context. First, Israel entered into a covenant relation with God at Sinai. The laws guided the people who were *already* in a covenant relation with Yahweh.

Of course, many of the laws are not directly relevant to the Christian. Many of the ceremonial laws were fulfilled in Christ. Many of the casuistic laws were legal codes for ancient Israel. The Christian exegete should first of all seek to understand the original meaning of the law. He or she should then look for relevant ethical or theological principles for today.

For example, the command not to reap to the edge of one's field (Lev 19:9-10) should not be taken literally today. But the ethical principle for us is that a person should be concerned for the poor and needy.

A law prescribing death for an adulterer (such as Lev 20:10) should not be applied literally in our secular country. But the ethical meaning for us is clear: adultery is wrong.

Ritual laws like those for the Day of Atonement (in Leviticus 16) are no longer normative for the Christian since Jesus was the final high priest and sacrifice. Instead, these laws look forward to Jesus Christ.

The laws of the Old Testament are relevant for the Christian if properly interpreted and applied.

Liturgical Literature

The Old Testament has songs and prayers that were used in the worship of Israel. The book of Psalms contains the majority of this literature. There are different types of psalms.

Individual and communal laments. More than one-third of the psalms are laments. In these psalms the Psalmist often describes his desperate situation and calls to God for help. These psalms have different elements: the complaint, the appeal for help, the reason or motivation, the confidence and the like. (Examples of individual psalms of lament are Psalms 3-7; Psalms 79 and 80 are communal laments.)

Psalms of thanksgiving. After the psalmist was rescued, he would sometimes write a psalm of thanksgiving. Elements in such psalms include a narrative of his deliverance, a call to thanksgiving and a vow to thank God. (Psalms 116 and 118 are examples. Jonah 2 is another example.)

Hymns. A hymn is a general song of praise. Often there are just two elements: the call to praise and the reason for praise. (Psalms 103 and 117 are examples.)

Psalms of confidence or trust. These psalms are really subcategories of the psalms of lament. Psalm 23 is an example; in the background of this psalm is the valley of the shadow of death which threatened the psalmist.

Royal psalms. These psalms celebrate an event in the life of the king. Psalms 2 and 110 are examples. They have possible messianic significance.

Liturgical psalms. These psalms describe or prescribe elements of temple worship. Psalm 24, example, may have been used when the ark was ritually brought into the temple. Psalm 118 reflects a temple liturgy.

A Christian exegete should first understand these psalms in their original context before applying them to his or her present life setting.

Prophecy

A large section of the Old Testament is prophecy. A prophet is one who speaks God's word. Sometimes prophecy is prediction of the future (foretelling). But usually prophecy is God's word for the present (forth-telling). God raised prophets in times of spiritual crisis in order to call God's people back to himself.[5]

Prophetic books are composed of oracles or individual prophecies. The first thing that an exegete should do in interpreting prophecies is to *"think oracles."*[6] One should identify the limits and the type of an oracle. There are three basic types of oracles.[7]

Oracle of judgment. An oracle of judgment brings judgment on the hearers because of their faithlessness and disobedience. The first two chapters of Amos have 9 oracles of judgment against the nations and against Israel and Judah.

---

[5]See T. Palmer, *A Theology of the Old Testament* (Bukuru: Africa Christian Textbooks, 2011), pp. 111-17.

[6]Fee and Stuart, *How To Read the Bible for All Its Worth*, p. 158.

[7]See H.D. Preuss, *Old Testament Theology* (Louisville: Westminster John Knox, 1992), 2:76-81.

Oracle of exhortation. An oracle of exhortation reminds the audience how to live. Jeremiah's plea for Israel to return to God and to repent (Jer 3:12-13) is an oracle of exhortation.

Oracle of salvation. Often after a word of judgment, the prophet will speak a word of hope. Such a word is an oracle of salvation. The final verses of Amos (9:11-15) are an oracle of salvation. Amos here predicts future salvation. Note that Amos here uses the future tense. Sometimes there is a multiple fulfillment—often at the return from exile, but more generally in the period of the church or beyond.

Old Testament prophecy is God's Word to Israel. Its relevance to the church today is often rather direct.

Wisdom Literature

Wisdom literature is a neglected part of the Bible. Old Testament wisdom literature includes Proverbs, Job, Ecclesiastes and some of the psalms (Pss 36, 37, 49, 73, 112, 127, 128, 133).[8]

Wisdom in the Old Testament is derived from practical experience.[9] One author defines biblical wisdom as "living life in God's world by God's rules."[10] There are at least four genres within wisdom literature.[11]

Proverbs

A proverb is "a concise, memorable statement of truth learned over extended human experience."[12] The African culture has many proverbs that teach general truths. The book of Proverbs especially has

---

[8]Fee and Stuart, *How To Read the Bible for All Its Worth*, pp. 187, 177.

[9]See T. Palmer, *A Theology of the Old Testament*, pp. 98-105.

[10]G. Osborne, *The Hermeneutical Spiral*, p. 242.

[11]W. Klein et al., *Introduction to Biblical Interpretation*, pp. 387-98.

[12]W. Klein et al., *Introduction to Biblical Interpretation*, p. 387.

many of these sayings. An example is: "Lazy hands make a person poor, but diligent hands bring wealth" (Prov 10:4).

Of course, such a statement is a generalization which is usually but not always true. Such a proverb comes first of all from human experience, not special revelation.

Instruction

Wisdom literature also contains direct instruction or teaching. An example is: "Do not move an ancient boundary stone set up by your forefathers" (Prov 22:28). Longer sections of instruction are found in the first nine chapters of Proverbs. This section is introduced by the words: "Listen, my son, to your father's instruction, and do not forsake your mother's teaching" (Prov 1:8).

Example Story and Reflection

These two types are autobiographical genres. In the example story the author records a personal experience that contains a lesson. For example, in Proverbs 24:30-34 the author passes by the field of a lazy man and is struck by the dangers of sloth.

The book of Ecclesiastes contains many reflections. The Teacher observed life and drew lessons from his observations. For example: "Again I looked and saw all the oppression that was taking place under the sun" (Eccl 4:1; cf. also 1:14; 3:16; 5:13, etc.).

Disputation Speeches

In a disputation speech, a person "seeks to persuade the audience of some truth."[13] The book of Job is full of such speeches.

One needs to be careful with such speeches in Job. The speeches of Job's so-called friends will have some bad theology—as do the speeches

---

[13]W. Klein et al., *Introduction to Biblical Interpretation*, p. 393.

of Satan. One needs to consider such speeches in the context of the entire book.

Gospel

In the New Testament, a prominent genre is Gospel. (The word "Gospel" is derived from the Greek word euangelion, which means "good news.")

Some scholars claim that the genre of the Gospels is biography, like the Hellenistic biography. But our Gospels are significantly different from Hellenistic biographies. Other scholars have suggested that the Gospels are theological biographies.[14] Other scholars agree with Justin Martyr who said that the Gospels are "the memoirs of the apostles."[15]

The Gospels are theological biographies of Jesus containing many of Jesus' sayings. The theological context of the Gospels is the arrival of the Kingdom of God.

The Gospels contain a few genres of literature.

Parables

About one third of the teachings of Jesus in the Synoptic Gospels are in the form of a parable. Popularly, parables are earthly stories with heavenly meanings.

Traditionally, the early and medieval church used a great deal of allegory in the interpretation of the parables. But Joachim Jeremias insisted that each parable has a single message. Yet we cannot rule out all allegory in the parables.[16]

One should remember the Kingdom context of the parables. One author suggested that a parable is an "encounter mechanism."

---

[14]W. Klein et al., *Introduction to Biblical Interpretation*, p. 401.

[15]Fee and Stuart, *How To Read the Bible for All Its Worth*, p. 105.

[16]G. Osborne, *The Hermeneutical Spiral*, pp. 291-94.

"The parables encounter, interpret and invite the listener/reader to participate in Jesus' new world vision of the kingdom."[17]

Narratives

Much of the Gospels is narrative. There are different sub-genres in the narratives. Scholars speak of miracle stories and pronouncement stories.[18] The Gospels present narratives to proclaim that Jesus is the Messiah and to proclaim the nature of the new Kingdom of God. The narratives are theological history.

Epistles

Letter writing is a common practice in most cultures. The New Testament contains 21 letters from the book of Romans to Jude. We call these letters epistles. The New Testament epistles are "genuine letters."[19]

The New Testament letters "are all . . . occasional documents" or letters.[20] In other words, they were written in a historical context responding to a historical situation.

Yet there is also a supracultural dimension to the epistles. Many of them were intended to be theological tracts or treatises for the early churches. They were meant to be read over and over again. Thus, "the New Testament Epistles fall between the private letter and the treatise."[21]

Hellenistic letters generally had six parts: the name of the writer; the name of the recipient; a greeting; a prayer wish or thanksgiving;

---

[17]G. Osborne, *The Hermeneutical Spiral*, pp. 295-96.

[18]See W. Klein et al., *Introduction to Biblical Interpretation*, pp. 415-18.

[19]M. Silva in *Introduction to Biblical Hermeneutics*, p. 174.

[20]Fee and Stuart, *How To Read the Bible for All Its Worth*, p. 45.

[21]G. Osborne, *The Hermeneutical Spiral*, p. 317.

the body; and the final greeting.[22] Most New Testament letters have the same structure.

A discerning exegete will notice if some of these elements are missing. For example, the thanksgiving is missing in the letter to the Galatians. That suggests that there was a serious problem in Galatia. Other letters like Hebrews and 1 John do not have the opening elements. This suggests that they were intended to be general epistles.

An exegete of the epistles should first of all consider the historical setting of the epistle; then the exegete should consider the main point of each paragraph or pericope.

Apocalyptic Literature

Apocalypse is a genre of literature common in the few centuries before and after Christ. Apocalyptic literature usually deals with the end of world history; visions, dreams and elaborate symbolism are common; battles between good and evil often happen; and God frequently intervenes in a supernatural way.[23]

Apocalyptic elements can be found in the books of Daniel and Zechariah, in the visions of Ezekiel 37-39 and other prophetic books, as well as in much intertestamental literature.[24]

The book of Revelation is a special case. On the one hand, "the Revelation is primarily an apocalypse."[25] But Revelation is also a letter (epistle) and a prophecy. Thus, "the book of Revelation is a composite of apocalyptic, prophetic and epistolary forms."[26]

---

[22]Fee and Stuart, *How To Read the Bible for All Its Worth*, p. 44.

[23]W. Klein et al., *Introduction to Biblical Interpretation*, p. 444.

[24]G. Osborne, *The Hermeneutical Spiral*, p. 275.

[25]Fee and Stuart, *How To Read the Bible for All Its Worth*, p. 206.

[26]G. Osborne, *The Hermeneutical Spiral*, p. 285.

Since Daniel and Revelation have large apocalyptic parts, the exegete should avoid interpreting these books too literally.

Knowledge of the genre of a passage will help one correctly interpret the passage since each genre has a different style of writing. It is appropriate in a research paper to make some general observations about the genre of your pericope.

Study Questions

1. How are the books of Kings theological or interpreted history?
2. What are casuistic laws and apodictic laws?
3. What are the genres of Psalms 3, 74, 100 and 118?
4. Is prophecy mostly a prediction of the future? Why or why not?
5. What are the three wisdom books in the Bible?
6. What is the genre of Philemon? What is the message of Philemon for us today?
7. What is the genre of the book of Revelation? How should we interpret it?

CHAPTER 6

GIVE THE LITERARY CONTEXT

The Bible contains some unusual statements. The Bible says: "There is no God" (Ps 14:1); "Let us eat and drink, for tomorrow we die" (1 Cor 15:32); and "you [Jesus] are a Samaritan and demon-possessed" (Jn 8:48).

These are genuine, literal statements from the Bible. But they are taken out of context. William Shakespeare once said: "The devil can cite Scripture for his purpose."[1]

It is important to consider the literary context of any passage to understand fully the meaning of the pericope.

A text is found in different layers of contexts. There is the immediate context, or the passages that come directly before and after the text. There is the book context. There is also the canonical context. We can picture this by putting the text in the center of a series of concentric circles.

In the above examples, the immediate context will tell you that the fool is the one who says that there is no God; the one who denies the resurrection will say that we should eat and drink without any concern

---

[1]William Shakespeare, "The Merchant of Venice"; quoted by M. Gorman in *Elements of Biblical Exegesis*, p. 69.

for the future; and the unbelieving Jews were the ones who thought that Jesus was demon-possessed.

> Literary criticism of biblical texts recognizes that a single text, passage, or pericope . . . generally forms a part of a larger whole —the document of which it is a part.[2]

As you consider the literary context, you should begin with the immediate context. What are the passages that are immediately before or after a text?

You should then place your text in the context of the entire Bible book. Why is your text placed where it is? To do this, it is useful to present a simple outline of the Bible book where your text is found.

For example, it is significant to note that the Ten Commandments in Exodus 20 are given in the context of the making of the covenant at Sinai. Law in the Old Testament is usually found in a covenantal context.

It is useful to know that the command to meditate on God's law (Josh 1:8) is found at the beginning of the book of Joshua. The theology of a book is often defined by the opening paragraphs.

It is helpful to note that the words "great is your faithfulness" (Lam 3:23) are found in the middle of the laments of Jeremiah in the book of Lamentations. Despite the complaints of Jeremiah, he still believed in God's faithfulness.

It is significant that the healing of the demon-possessed man in Mark 5 comes before Peter's confession of Jesus as the Messiah. The first half of Mark proclaims Jesus as the Messiah; the second half of Mark teaches the suffering mission of the Messiah.

---

[2]Hayes and Holladay, *Biblical Exegesis*, p. 94.

It is important to realize that Jesus' statement "I am the bread of life" (Jn 6:35) is made in the context of the feeding of bread to the five thousand people.

It is significant that the command to be kind to one another (Eph 4:32) is found in the practical second half of the book of Ephesians, after the more theological first half of the epistle.

It is important to understand the literary structure of the book of Revelation in order to fully understand the millennial passage of Revelation 20. One commentator for example believes that this passage should be seen in parallelism with the seven seals, seven trumpets and seven bowls.[3]

Finally, one should remember the canonical context.

> For those who read the Bible theologically, one of the contexts within which a text may be considered is the Bible, or the canon, as a whole—the canonical context.[4]

How does your text relate to the rest of Scripture? Are there other texts in Scripture that support your interpretation of your text? Does your text stand in tension with other texts? Can this tension be resolved?

"Considering the canonical context allows the exegete to put biblical texts in conversation with one another."[5] Probably, though, this theological conversation will occur at the end of your exegesis, as you seek to determine the theological meaning of your text.

One writer concludes: "A text without a context . . . is a potentially dangerous weapon."[6] It is important to give sufficient attention to the immediate literary context and the broader context of your text.

---

[3] Wm. Hendriksen, *More Than Conquerors* (Grand Rapids: Baker, 1939).
[4] M. Gorman, *Elements of Biblical Exegesis*, p. 78.
[5] M. Gorman, *Elements of Biblical Exegesis*, p. 78.
[6] M. Gorman, *Elements of Biblical Exegesis*, p. 79.

Study Questions

1. Describe the different levels of the literary context of a text.
2. Describe the literary context of Jonah's prayer in the second chapter of Jonah.
3. Describe the literary context of Psalm 22:12.
4. Describe the literary context of "Out of Egypt I have called my son" in Hosea 11:1 and Matthew 2:15.
5. Describe the literary context of Colossians 3:2.
6. Describe the literary context of "You are a priest forever, in the order of Melchizedek" (Heb 7:17).

CHAPTER 7

DO A WORD STUDY

A text consists of words. To exegete a text, one has to know the meaning of these words.

So what is a word? A word is an arbitrary sign with meaning. "A word is a semantic sign—a combination of symbols or sounds that represents an idea."[1] Words take on meaning as they are used. Usage determines the meaning of a word.

As we consider words, we note that a word does not always have one single meaning. "A biblical word . . . does not mean the same thing in every place it occurs."[2]

Instead, words have a range of meanings. The *semantic range* of a word is the "spectrum of possible meanings" of a word.[3]

Consider, for example, the Greek word *kosmos* (world). At least three main meanings of *kosmos* can be found in the Greek New Testament.[4] At times *kosmos* is the created, physical world (e.g., Jn 17:5). In other places *kosmos* refers to all of humanity (e.g., Jn 18:20),

---

[1] W. Klein et al., *Introduction to Biblical Interpretation*, p. 241.

[2] M. Gorman, *Elements of Biblical Exegesis*, p. 108.

[3] M. Gorman, *Elements of Biblical Exegesis*, p. 106.

[4] See T. Palmer, *A Theology of the New Testament* (Bukuru: Africa Christian Textbooks, 2012), pp. 47-48.

Often, however, *kosmos* is those people who are not believers (e.g., Jn 7:7).

There is thus a semantic range for the word *kosmos*. This Greek word has a range of meanings. A word study should describe the semantic range of the selected word.

So how do we know the meaning of a word in a particular verse? It is the context which will determine the meaning. "The meaning of a word . . . depends upon a combination of the dictionary meaning and the context."[5]

If, for example, the Pharisees complain that the whole world (*kosmos*) has gone after Jesus (Jn 12:19), this world is not the physical created world nor only the unbelievers but rather all the people in the Palestinian region. In this case, the context of the word is decisive in understanding the meaning of the word.

Another example would be the Greek word for salvation (*soteria*). The song of Zechariah (Lk 1:68-79) is a single pericope containing three occurrences of *soteria*. In Luke 1:71, *soteria* is deliverance from enemies; in Luke 1:77, *soteria* is salvation through the forgiveness of sins. But what is *soteria* in the "horn of salvation" of Luke 1:69? The immediate context of this phrase and the broader context of the New Testament and the Old Testament will be decisive in interpreting this phrase.

A concordance is thus important in doing word studies. How often does the Hebrew or Greek word occur in the Bible book you are studying? How often does this word occur in the Old or New Testament? How is this word used throughout Scripture?

Ideally, a Hebrew or Greek concordance should be used. Alternatively, a traditional English concordance to a literal version of the Bible could be used.

---

[5]M. Gorman, *Elements of Biblical Exegesis*, p. 108.

One should be warned at this point against the misuse of etymology.[6] Theological dictionaries often speculate about the origins of a Hebrew or Greek word. Such historical studies may be interesting but are not an infallible guide to the current meaning of a word.

Consider, for example, the English word "sincere." This word comes from the Latin words "without wax." A sincere statue or sincere honey did not have wax. While this may be historically interesting, wax is not part of the current meaning of "sincere."[7]

> Etymology . . . gives a false idea of the nature of a vocabulary for it is concerned only in showing how a vocabulary has been formed. Words are not used according to their historical value. . . . Words always have a *current* value.[8]

The meaning of a word depends on the current usage of the word and not on its historical origins. The meaning of a particular word depends on the context in which it is found. Word studies will help an exegete to understand the meaning of particular words in their context.

---

[6]See G. Osborne, *The Hermeneutical Spiral*, pp. 87-89.

[7]See M. Silva in *Introduction to Biblical Hermeneutics*, pp. 55-56.

[8]J. Vendrye, Language: *A Linguistic Introduction to History*; quoted by G. Osborne, The Hermeneutical Spiral, p. 88.

Study Questions

1. What is a word?
2. What is the semantic range of a word?
3. How can we find out the meaning of an individual word in a particular text?
4. Describe the limitations of etymological studies.
5. Why are concordances important when doing word studies?

CHAPTER 8

GIVE THE STRUCTURE AND ANALYSIS OF THE TEXT

Exegesis is more than just a series of word studies. How do the words in a text relate to each other? What is the main message of the text?

Syntax describes how words in a sentence relate to each other. In the narrow sense, syntax is "the relationship between the words of a sentence." In the broad sense, syntax is "all the interrelationships within the sentence as a means of determining the meaning of the unit as a whole."[1]

In the narrow sense, syntax deals mostly with grammar. In the broader sense, syntax deals with the structure of the sentence or the paragraph. Grammar and structure are two basic considerations in exegeting a text.

Some exegetes recommend creating an outline to understand the structure of a text. Stuart says: "Try to construct an outline that genuinely represents the major units of information."[2] Fee suggests making a sentence flow or a sentence diagram.[3] Such an outline or

---

[1] G. Osborne, *The Hermeneutical Spiral*, p. 113.
[2] D. Stuart, *Old Testament Exegesis*, p. 15.
[3] G. Fee, *New Testament Exegesis*, p. 13.

diagram will indicate the main clause or clauses and the subordinate clause or clauses in a sentence.

For example, Psalm 117 has two imperatives in parallelism followed by a two-part subordinate clause, after which is a final imperative. An outline or sentence diagram would look like this:

> *Psalm 117*
> Praise Yahweh, all you nations;
> extol him, all you peoples,
>
> > for great is his love toward us,
> > and the faithfulness of Yahweh endures forever.
>
> Praise Yahweh.

The main thought of the Psalm is clear: Israel is called to praise God. The reason for this command is found in the subordinate clauses: for (*ki*) Yahweh is loving and faithful. The sentence diagram helps us to visualize the structure of the text.

Another example comes from Amos. Amos 9:11-12 has four imperfect verbs in parallelism referring to future action, followed by a purpose clause and a messenger formula. An outline or diagram might be:

> *Amos 9:11-12*
> I will restore David's fallen tent in that day,
> and I will repair its broken places,
> and I will restore its ruins,
> and I will build it as it used to be,
>
> > so that they may possess the remnant of Edom
> > > and all the nations that bear my name,
>
> declares Yahweh who will do these things.

This outline suggests the future activity of Yahweh and the purpose for this intended action.

A longer pericope like Psalm 3 does not necessarily have to be written out in its entirety, but the structure is reasonably clear.

Psalm 3

Vss 1-2:	complaint (or lament)
Vss 3-4:	trust (or confidence)
Vss 5-6:	trust (or confidence)
Vs 7:	call for help and reason
Vs 8:	trust and final prayer.

An outline for this psalm of lament suggests movement or a flow of thought. The psalmist begins with his complaint embedded in an attitude of trust. He concludes with the appeal for help. The main thought is the appeal for help.

The flow of a narrative is sometimes more difficult to ascertain. But a possible flow of thought or outline of Genesis 11:1-9 might look like this:

Genesis 11:1-9

Vss 1-2:	the setting
Vss 3-4:	the action of the people
Vss 5-8:	the response of Yahweh
Vs 9:	consequence.

In this small passage, the setting is given; the drama builds up; Yahweh's action forms the climax of the story; and then the consequences are delineated. A narrative analysis like this reminds us that the main point of the narrative is Yahweh's critical response to human pride.

The outline of the historical narrative of the feeding of the 5000 might look like this:

Matthew 14:13-21

Vss 13-14:	the setting
Vss 15-17:	the problem of no food
Vss 18-19:	Jesus' response in providing food
Vss 20-21:	the consequence

One can see from this outline how the drama builds up to a climax when Jesus feeds the five thousand. The main point of this miracle story is the power of Jesus to provide for the needs of people.

A detailed outline of a Pauline passage will need to consult a literal translation of the Greek itself, since contemporary translations like the NIV tend to break longer sentences into shorter ones. Consider, for example, the single Greek sentence of Ephesians 5:18-21. An outline based on the Greek text and the English Standard Version (ESV) would look like this:

Ephesians 5:18-21
And do not get drunk with wine, in which is debauchery,
but be filled with the Spirit,

    speaking to one another in psalms and hymns and
        spiritual songs,
    singing

> and making melody to the Lord with your heart,
> giving thanks always and for everything to God the
> Father in the name of our Lord Jesus Christ,
> submitting to one another out of reverence for Christ.

The structure of this passage is reasonably clear. The single Greek sentence has two imperatives followed by five participles. Probably the main thought of the pericope would be the positive command to be filled with the Holy Spirit. The five participles provide additional instructions to the believer.

Often the main thought of the author is found in the main clause of a sentence, although at times the main thought will be in subordinate clauses. Note in the example above how the final participial phrase ("submitting to one another out of reverence for Christ") introduces the next section of husband-wife relations. Some translations even make this last participial phrase a new sentence, and sometimes even part of a new paragraph.

It is useful to identify subordinate clauses. Adverbial clauses answer basic questions. The following is a full list of adverbial subordinate clauses and the question answered: temporal clauses (when?), local clauses (where?), causal clauses (why?), purpose clauses (why?), result clauses (why?), conditional clauses (when?), concessive clauses (how?) and comparative clauses (how?).[4]

Once the structure of the passage has been established, the exegete will then need to analyze the text, paying attention to significant grammatical details and the general flow of the text.

The purpose of this entire exercise is to hear what the author is saying. What is the message of the text for the original audience?

---

[4]W. Klein et al., *Introduction to Biblical Interpretation*, p. 267.

Study Questions

1.   Why is exegesis more than word studies?
2.   What is syntax?
3.   Describe the structure of Psalm 95.
4.   Construct an outline to describe the flow of thought of Genesis 28:10-22.
5.   Construct an outline of Philippians 2:12-13 noting the main clause and the subordinate clauses.
6.   Construct an outline of 1 Peter 2:9-10 noting the main clause and the subordinate clause.
7.   Construct an outline to describe the flow of thought of Acts 3:1-11.

CHAPTER 9

SUGGEST THE MEANING OF THE TEXT

The goal of interpretation is to understand the meaning of the text. At the end of the exegetical process, you should state what you think the meaning of the text is.

This final step is called the *synthesis*. "To synthesize is to pull various elements together into some kind of unified whole. Synthesizing, then, is a disciplined but creative act of integration."[1]

At the end of the exegetical activity, you should state what you think the main point is. As Prof. J. Christiaan Beker asked of every text in every class at Princeton Seminary, "What is the punch line?"[2]

You should then explain the full meaning of the text as you see it. Of course, your interpretation of the text may not be the only one. But you should prayerfully set forth your own interpretation "with vigor, but also with humility."[3]

In this process, one should not neglect the broader canonical context. We believe that all of Scripture comes from God and is

---

[1] M. Gorman, *Elements of Biblical Exegesis*, p. 127.
[2] M. Gorman, *Elements of Biblical Exegesis*, p. 127.
[3] M. Gorman, *Elements of Biblical Exegesis*, p. 129.

authoritative. How does the message of our passage fit into the broader canonical context?

We should then listen to other biblical passages relating to our own passage. But at the same time we should allow the distinctive message of our own passage to be heard.

The purpose of the exegetical process is to hear God speaking to us through the words of Scripture. At the end of the exegetical exercise, we should be able

> to hear the voice of God speaking once again through the words of Scripture when they are read with care and in dependence on the Spirit who inspired those words and continues to breathe life into them.[4]

Study Questions

1. Why is the end of the exegetical process called synthesis?
2. Explain the canonical dimension of the exegesis of a text.
3. What is the original meaning of Psalm 117?
4. What is the original meaning of Mark 8:27-30?
5. What is the original meaning of Ephesians 6:1-4?

---

[4]M. Gorman, *Elements of Biblical Exegesis*, p. 136.

CHAPTER 10

APPLY THE TEXT TO THE AFRICAN SITUATION

The Bible is a "sacred text" which is normative for our faith and life.[1] The Bible is God's Word for our lives. Paul says that all Scripture "is useful for teaching, rebuking, correcting and training in righteousness" (2 Tim 3:16).

Thus,

> the study of Scripture can never be complete until one has moved from text to context. . . . Scripture should not merely be learned; it must be believed and then proclaimed.[2]

Another scholar said:

> The final goal of exegesis is actualization, or embodiment —living the text. The ultimate goal of exegesis is for the individual and community to become a living exegesis of the text.[3]

---

[1]Hayes and Holladay, *Biblical Exegesis*, p. 191.
[2]G. Osborne, *The Hermeneutical Spiral*, p. 410.
[3]M. Gorman, *Elements of Biblical Exegesis*, p. 160.

In other words, the text needs to be applied to our present-day situation. But this is problematic. The Bible books were written thousands of years ago in a completely different culture than ours.

Scholars today talk of two horizons of a text. The first horizon is the original context of the text; the second horizon is our contemporary setting. For a text to be meaningful to us, the two horizons need to be brought together—without obscuring the separate significance of each.

So how is this done? How is the gap between the two horizons bridged?

To make a text relevant we need to listen carefully to the text. What does the text tell us about God, mankind, God's salvation, our responsibilities, God's people and the world? *"In a word, what claims about God, and about God's claim on us, does the text make?"*[4]

One writer calls for *spiritual exegesis* after pursuing the grammatico-historical procedure. The historical-critical method of interpretation is scientific but often dry and arid. We need the Holy Spirit to apply the text to our lives. This requires humility, personalizing Scripture, praying Scripture, meditation, listening prophetically, mirroring and imaginative application.[5]

The danger of spiritual exegesis—and application in general—is subjectivism. Frequently a preacher will use a text to support his own theology or agenda. But the abuse should not remove the imperative of applying the text to our contemporary situation.

As we reflect on the relevance of Scripture for our lives, we need to remember that many of the commands and admonitions in Scripture are culture-bound and time-bound.

---

[4]M. Gorman, *Elements of Biblical Exegesis*, p. 162.
[5]D. Deppe, *All Roads Lead to the Text*, pp. 262-91.

For example: "Do not plant your field with two kinds of seed" (Lev 19:19); "greet one another with a holy kiss" (1 Cor 16:20); "I also want women to dress modestly, with decency and propriety, not with braided hair or gold or pearls or expensive clothes" (1 Tim 2:9).

In such cases, the exegete needs to distinguish between the cultural and the supracultural elements of a passage. What is the lasting or eternal principle that the passage teaches?[6]

As one looks for the application of a text, one needs to remember the canonical context. Old Testament passages, for example, need to be seen in the light of the New Testament.

The book of Joshua, for example, tells of God's commands to Joshua and Israel to conquer Canaan. Does the book of Joshua recommend holy war for us today? Probably not. Instead, the New Testament speaks of the spiritual warfare between the kingdom of God and the kingdom of Satan.

John Bright says that

> the theology of Joshua—the promise, the battle, and the victory —has been caught up in the New Testament and given a new and profounder meaning in Christ. . . . *These very texts* speak to us through Christ in their own right and give us a word of their own that we very much need to hear.[7]

Bright says that "the preacher must . . . bring his [Old Testament] text to the New Testament, as it were, for verdict." But his message should still be an Old Testament sermon. Bright believes that "every Old Testament text, if rightly heard, has its word for us today."[8] The exegete should seek to find this word.

---

[6]See G. Osborne, *The Hermeneutical Spiral*, pp. 420-26.

[7]J. Bright, *The Authority of the Old Testament*, p. 248.

[8]J. Bright, *The Authority of the Old Testament*, pp. 211-12.

God's Word is relevant and normative for us today. The exegete should listen to hear this word. The believer should apply this word to his or her life. The preacher should bring God's Word to his people.

Study Questions

1. What is the final goal of exegesis?
2. What are the two horizons of a text?
3. How do we merge the two horizons?
4. What is spiritual exegesis?
5. What is the relevance to us of Leviticus 16 and its prescriptions for the Day of Atonement?
6. What is the relevance of the oracle of judgment against Edom in Amos 1:11-12?
7. What is the relevance of the healing of the blind man in Mark 8:22-26?
8. What is the relevance of the book of Philemon for the Christian today?

PART III

A BRIEF HISTORY OF INTERPRETATION

If you stand on the shoulders of giants, you can see further. It is useful to consider the history of exegesis in order to learn from the theological giants that have gone before us.

This is a brief history of exegesis of the Bible in the last two thousand years.

Jesus and The Apostles

Our study of the history of exegesis begins with Jesus. The scriptures for him were the Old Testament.

It is evident first of all that the Old Testament scriptures were absolutely authoritative for Jesus. Jesus often appealed to the Old Testament as an authority in life and in doctrine.

At the beginning of Jesus' ministry, Satan tempted Jesus three times. Jesus responded with the words "it is written" followed by an Old Testament passage (Mt 4:1-11; Lk 4:1-13). Jesus used the Old Testament as an authority in his debate with Satan.

(It should be noted that Satan too used Scripture for his own purposes. We see that Scripture can easily be misused by misguided persons.)

Jesus assumed that the Old Testament had both a divine author and human authors. Once in a debate with the Jewish leaders, Jesus said that "David himself speaking by the Holy Spirit" spoke the words of Psalm 110 (Mk 12:36).

In another debate, Jesus said that "the Scripture cannot be broken" (Jn 10:35). Jesus assumed the divine authority of the Old Testament.

Jesus believed that the Old Testament scriptures were a guide for life and doctrine. When asked which commandment was the most important, Jesus quoted the commands from the Torah to love God and to love one's neighbor. In this debate Jesus also reaffirmed the Torah's confession that God is one (Mk 12:29-31).

In the Sermon on the Mount, Jesus gave a spiritual interpretation to the Ten Commandments. The commands not to murder and not to commit adultery, for example, should be internalized. Murder and adultery also include the internal sins of hate and lust (Mt 5:21-30).

In a broader sense, Jesus assumed that the Old Testament pointed to himself as the Messiah. Jesus' ministry began with the words: "The time is fulfilled (*peplērōtai*) and the kingdom of God is near" (Mk 1:15). The Old Testament has its fulfillment in Jesus.

The same idea is expressed in Jesus' first sermon at Nazareth. After reading part of Isaiah 61, Jesus said, "Today this scripture is fulfilled in your hearing" (Lk 4:20-21).

On the road to Emmaus, Jesus said that the Law of Moses and the prophets pointed to himself (Lk 24:27). He said, "Everything must be fulfilled that is written about me in the Law of Moses, the Prophets and the Psalms" (Lk 24:44). "Then he opened their minds so they could understand the Scriptures" (Lk 24:45).

A vital hermeneutical key for Jesus is that all of the Old Testament pointed to himself as the Messiah. To use contemporary language, Jesus' understanding of the Old Testament was deeply christological.

Jesus' understanding of the Old Testament shaped the apostles' view of scripture. For them Jesus is the fulfillment of all of the Old Testament.

We can see this clearly in Matthew's Gospel. Old Testament texts like "out of Egypt I called my son" (Hos 11:1) or "a voice is heard in Ramah, mourning and great weeping" (Jer 31:15) are applied to Jesus (Mt 2:15,18).

Matthew's reading of these Old Testament texts is not literal. But Matthew, like Jesus, was a Jew and he used Jewish rabbinic methods to demonstrate his main point that Jesus is the Messiah.

The same hermeneutical methods are used by Paul and the other New Testament writers. For example, in Ephesians 4:8-10 Paul gives a christological interpretation to a text from the Psalms which describes Yahweh's entrance into Zion in triumph.

Jesus and the apostles were Jews who used Jewish exegetical methods for interpreting Scripture. But most of us are not Jewish. Since we are not Jews we should be careful about using Jewish exegetical methods. But we gladly accept the main theological point: Jesus is the fulfillment of the hopes of Old Testament Israel.[9]

Second-century Exegesis

The second century (AD 100 to 199) was a dynamic period for the church. All sorts of good and bad doctrines were being taught in Christian circles.

"Christian" Gnosticism said that physical matter was bad and that the Old Testament creator was a bad God since he made matter. Many Gnostics then rejected the Old Testament. They also rejected the incarnation since they thought that human flesh is evil.

---

[9]See R. Longenecker, *Biblical Exegesis in the Apostolic Period* (Grand Rapids: Eerdmans, 1999), pp. 185-98.

Marcion was a lay theologian who had similar ideas as the Gnostics. He too rejected the Old Testament because he thought it was too physical.

So what was true? The early church said that if something was apostolic, it was true since the apostles were closest to Jesus. They concluded that the apostolic creed (like the Apostles' Creed), the apostolic writings (the New Testament books) and the apostolic succession (bishops in the line of the apostles) were a guarantee of the truth.[10]

By the end of the second century, there was basic agreement on which books were part of the New Testament canon. The so-called Gnostic Gospels were rejected by the early church as being not authentic or truly apostolic.

Bishop Irenaeus was important in this process. He became bishop of Lyons around AD 180. He wrote books against the Gnostics, complaining about their poor exegetical methodology. The Gnostics neglected the context of Bible passages and used isolated passages and words to support their speculative theories. Also, they interpreted clear and obvious texts in dark and obscure ways.[11] Irenaeus argued for a more direct and responsible method of exegesis.

To control theology Irenaeus appealed to the apostolic church. He said:

> True knowledge is the teaching of the apostles, and the ancient order of the Church in all the world, and the form of the body of Christ according to the successions of bishops . . . .[12]

---

[10]See H. Boer, *Early Church History* (Ibadan: Daystar, 1976), pp. 67-78.

[11]R. Grant and D. Tracy, *A Short History of the Interpretation of the Bible* (Minneapolis: Fortress, 1984), p. 49.

[12]Irenaeus, *Against Heresies*, 4.33.8, quoted by Grant and Tracy in *A Short History of the Interpretation of the Bible*, p. 50.

Irenaeus had great respect for the authority of Scripture. But because of the Gnostic crisis, Irenaeus insisted that Christian teaching and exegesis should conform to the authority of the church. In a sense, this is a worrying development. Should the church control how we read the Bible?

Alexandria and Antioch

The Old Testament has passages that are difficult for a Christian. The Torah commands blood sacrifices. The book of Joshua talks about holy wars. The book of Psalms has imprecatory psalms. Chronicles has long genealogies. So what is the spiritual relevance of these passages? Should these passages be allegorized?

Alexandria was a cosmopolitan city in Egypt at the mouth of the Nile. The Greek language and philosophy were strong in Alexandria. In this context the Alexandrian theologians resorted to allegory to interpret much of the Bible.

Clement of Alexandria was a theologian from Egypt who lived and worked around AD 200. He said that a Bible text can have different possible meanings: a historical sense, a doctrinal sense, a prophetic sense, a philosophical sense and a mystical sense. Scripture, he claimed, is written in symbols. The true meaning of a text is not usually the historical or literal meaning. Often the true meaning is the spiritual or allegorical sense.[13]

Thus Noah's ark would be a symbol or type of the church; Rahab's red cord would be a symbol of the saving blood of Jesus; Joshua's wars should be interpreted as the Christian's spiritual warfare with Satan.

Origen of Alexandria (ca. 182-254) followed Clement in his allegorization. Origen claimed that since Scripture is a spiritual document, it should be interpreted spiritually or allegorically. He says

---

[13]Grant and Tracy, *A Short History of the Interpretation of the Bible*, pp. 55-56.

that an exegete should decide whether the literal meaning of a text is the true meaning. All of Scripture has a spiritual sense, and not necessarily a literal sense.[14]

Clement and Origen contextualized the Gospel into their Greek philosophical context. Allegorization was a means to make the message of Scripture more acceptable to their Greek-Egyptian context. But is it good to abandon the literal historical interpretation of Scripture?

The theologians in Antioch thought this was not good. Antioch of Syria was a large city just north of Palestine. The historical events of the Old and New Testaments occurred close by. The theologians of Antioch assumed the historical and literal meaning of a text. For the most part they rejected allegorization.

For example, Theodore, bishop of Mopsuestia from 392 to 428, thought that Psalm 22 should be understood as a literal psalm of lament by the psalmist and not as a messianic prophecy. Theodore also understood the Song of Solomon to be a love song and not a spiritual allegory of the love between Christ and the church.

John Chrysostom, bishop of Constantinople until 407, preferred to use typology instead of allegory. Jerome (331-420) also insisted on the literal and historical meaning of a text.

Augustine and the Middle Ages

Augustine of Hippo (354-430) was the great Latin theologian of North Africa. The qualifications of a good exegete for him are: 1) to be filled with the love of God and one's neighbor; 2) to know the Bible well in Hebrew and Greek; 3) to be able to distinguish the literal and spiritual meanings of Scripture.[15]

---

[14]Grant and Tracy, *A Short History of the Interpretation of the Bible*, pp. 56-59.
[15]J. Preus, *Reading the Bible through Christ*, p. 40.

"Augustine was a master of allegorical interpretation."[16] His allegory of the Good Samaritan is striking: the man is Adam; Jerusalem is the heavenly city; Jericho is the moon and human mortality; the thieves are Satan and his demons; the wounded man is the sinner who lost his immortality; the priest and Levite are the Old Testament law; the Good Samaritan is Jesus; the binding of the wounds is the restraint of sin; oil is good hope; wine is the exhortation to work; the donkey is the flesh of Christ; sitting on the donkey is faith in Christ; the inn is the church; the two pieces of money are the two sacraments; and the innkeeper is the apostle Paul.[17]

This is an enormously creative and spiritual interpretation of Jesus' parable. But is this the real meaning of the text? Is this the literal meaning of the text of the parable? Are we hearing the word of God or the word of Augustine?

The great theologian Augustine thus gave his approval to a multiple sense of the text. The medieval church continued what Augustine and Alexandria started.

The Middle Ages in Europe is the thousand years between AD 500 and 1500. During this time the authority of the pope in Rome and the clergy increased. The medieval church assumed that the lay person cannot understand Scripture. So the western church said that the church will decide the proper meaning of Scripture. There were then two authorities for life and doctrine: Scripture and church tradition.

The medieval church said that a text might have four different meanings: the literal or historical; the allegorical or spiritual; the moral or ethical; and the anagogical or eschatological meaning. Thus Jerusalem could be: historically, a city in Palestine; allegorically, the

---

[16]J. Preus, *Reading the Bible through Christ*, p. 40.

[17]See J. Preus, *Reading the Bible through Christ*, pp. 40-41, quoting from Hayes and Holladay, *Biblical Exegesis*, pp. 18-19.

church; morally, the human soul; and eschatologically, the heavenly city.[18]

Even though the great medieval theologian Thomas Aquinas (1225-1274) recognized the foundational importance of the literal sense, he still allowed the other senses.

The Middle Ages in Europe was a time of great spirituality but also a time of superstition, corruption and theological confusion. The Word of God was often suppressed by the church. There was the need for a reformation in the church.

The Reformation

Martin Luther (1483-1546) was born and raised in the medieval Catholic Church. In his youth he never had access to a Bible. But as a lecturer in the University of Wittenberg he finally came to an awareness of the power and authority of Scripture. His famous principle was *sola Scriptura* (only Scripture): only Scripture was the final authority in faith and doctrine.

At his trial before the Emperor in the city of Worms, Luther said that since popes and councils have erred, "I am bound to the Scriptures . . . and my conscience is captive to the Word of God. . . . Here I stand."[19]

Luther believed in the *perspicuity* or clarity of Scripture. He believed that the essential doctrines of the Bible can be read and understood by the ordinary person. For this reason he translated the Bible into the vernacular German for his own people.

But if Scripture is to speak to us, it must speak with a clear voice. The clear voice of Scripture had been obscured by the multiple meanings imposed on the text. Luther complained:

---

[18]Grant and Tracy, *A Short History of Interpretation*, p. 85.

[19]S. Nichols, *Martin Luther* (Philippsburg: P&R, 2002), p. 42.

> When I was a monk, I was an expert in allegories. I allegorized
> everything. Afterward through the Epistle to the Romans I
> came to some knowledge of Christ.[20]

Luther complained that Origen ignored the grammatical sense and allegorized everything. But Luther insisted that

> no violence [be] done to the words of God, whether by man or
> angel. They are to be retained in their simplest meaning as far
> as possible. Unless the context manifestly compels it, they are
> not to be understood apart from their grammatical and proper
> sense.[21]

John Calvin (1509-1564) also complained that Origen twisted Scripture "away from the genuine sense," thinking that "the literal sense is too meager and poor." Origen thought that Scripture "is fertile and thus bears multiple meanings." But, Calvin wrote: "Let us know that the true meaning of Scripture is the natural and simple one, and let us embrace and hold it resolutely."[22]

The Protestant Reformation thus inaugurated the grammatico-historical method of exegesis as a method of finding the single meaning of a Bible text.

Reason and Faith After the Reformation

European theology after the Reformation was often characterized by an excessive use of reason. Of course reason is important in theology. But when reason surpasses faith, then we stand in danger of losing our faith.

---

[20]M. Luther, *Table Talk* (*Luther's Works*, vol. 54), p. 46.

[21]M. Luther, "The Babylonian Captivity of the Church," in *Luther's Works*, 36:30.

[22]J. Calvin, *Commentary on Galatians* (4:21-22), trans. T.H.L. Parker (Grand Rapids: Eerdmans, 1965), pp. 84-85.

The 18th century in Europe was the Age of Reason. But the excessive use of reason was already felt in the 17th century and continued into the 19th century. During this period many theologians and philosophers denied the miracles, the divine nature of Christ and the divine inspiration of the Bible. The Bible was simply a human book to many of these people. A few examples will illustrate this trend.[23]

In 1651 Thomas Hobbes in his *Leviathan* denied that God spoke directly through the Bible. He denied that the Bible is God's revelation; instead he thought it to be a record of God's revelation in history.

In 1670 the Jewish philosopher Baruch Spinoza claimed that "the Bible leaves reason absolutely free." Since the Bible does not speak authoritatively to us, we should study it solely for historical reasons.

In 1799 Schleiermacher rejected the absolute authority of the Bible. He also questioned many of the historical events in Jesus' life like the resurrection.

In England, Samuel Coleridge and Matthew Arnold rejected biblical inspiration. In America and England, biblical criticism was widely practiced.

It is in this context that the historical criticism of the Bible arose. Towards the end of the 19th century, Julius Wellhausen formulated his documentary hypothesis of the Old Testament. He posited the so-called Jahwist, Elohist, Deuteronomist and Priestly (J,E,D,P) sources of the Torah. But like Darwin's theory of evolution, this is an unproven hypothesis.

The 19th century came to a close with Prof. Adolf Harnack's lectures in Berlin where he denied the miracles, the incarnation of Jesus, the substitutionary atonement and the divine inspiration of the Bible. Harnack's theology is a classic statement of 19th century liberalism.

---

[23]See Grant and Tracy, *A Short History of the Interpretation of the Bible*, pp. 104-118.

It is interesting to note a link between biblical criticism and liberal theology. "The nineteenth-century critical movement . . . stood for liberalism in theology. . . . The two were closely connected."[24]

Of course, not all European theology in these centuries rejected the authority of the Bible. In the 17th century, Reformed and Lutheran orthodoxy held to the infallibility of the Bible. The Puritans in England at this time had an experiential Christianity. John Bunyan's *Pilgrim's Progress* is an example of this.

In Germany in the 18th century, the Pietists believed in the central doctrines of the Bible and they practiced an experiential Christianity. In England, John Wesley and the Evangelicals held to the central doctrines of Christianity.

In the 20th century, Karl Barth reacted to liberalism and reemphasized the authority of the Word of God. But he did not believe that the Bible was necessarily the Word of God. Instead, he thought that the Bible contains the Word of God and can become the Word of God.

But the world-wide Evangelical movement of the present time reaffirmed the authority of Scripture and the historic doctrines of the Bible.

Postmodernism

In recent decades there has been a crisis in biblical interpretation. All the assumptions of biblical interpretation are now being questioned by the postmodernists. The focus of interpretation is shifting from the text to the reader. The question is: does the text or the reader determine the meaning of a text?

Hans-Georg Gadamer's book *Truth and Method* is one of the first statements of postmodernism. In this book Gadamer says that every

---

[24]Grant and Tracy, *A Short History of the Interpretation of the Bible*, pp. 117-18.

text has two horizons: the horizon of the text and the horizon of the interpreter. Interpretation is a *fusion of the two horizons*.[25]

Interpretation, he thinks, is a dialogue between the text and the interpreter. Gadamer calls it a "game of conversation."[26] The text impacts the reader and the reader brings his or her world into the text. The two horizons are fused to create a new and contemporary meaning of the text. "The past (the text) and the present (the interpreter) merge."[27]

Thus, the primary meaning of a text for him is not its original meaning but "the common subject matter of both text and interpreter." Interpreters should not just seek for the original meaning of the text; instead, he thinks, they should translate or "interpret the meaning into their present horizon."[28]

Gadamer's theory is an interesting attempt to make the text relevant to today. But, as we suggested in the first part of this book, he blurs the distinction between the original meaning of a text and its application or personal meaning. The end result is pure subjectivism.

One writer observes that Gadamer's theory

> does not develop a method for distinguishing true from false interpretation. . . . Furthermore, he has an uncritical view of the role of the reader in interpretation. . . . Anarchy could easily be the result.[29]

Many types of postmodernism followed Gadamer. The reader-response school is one. Reader-response criticism is reader-centered instead of text-centered. In the end, the reader, not the text, determines

[25]G. Osborne, *The Hermeneutical Spiral*, pp. 469-70.
[26]Grant and Tracy, *A Short History of the Interpretation of the Bible*, pp. 158-60.
[27]G. Osborne, *The Hermeneutical Spiral*, p. 470.
[28]Grant and Tracy, *A Short History of the Interpretation of the Bible*, pp. 159-60.
[29]G. Osborne, *The Hermeneutical Spiral*, p. 471.

the meaning of a text. But if there are many readers of a text, then the text will have many different meanings.

Stanley Fish is a representative of this school. Fish posits "an ontological union between the reader and the text. In other words, the text disappears and the reader 'creates' meaning."[30]

The reader-response people suggest reading communities. When a group of people read the same text together, each person will have his own meaning for a text.

This may be an interesting exercise. But in the end Scripture loses its prophetic power. In the end, we will hear the voice of the person sitting next to us instead of the voice of the Lord.[31]

Global Hermeneutics

The end of the 20th century and the beginning of the 21st century have seen a dramatic rise in non-western theologies and methods of hermeneutics. We can highlight only a few examples here.

Liberation theology arose in the 1960s in Latin America. The context was socio-economic and political injustice. Liberation theology stressed the social or horizontal dimension of salvation.

Liberation theology came to Africa in the 1970s. Black theology in South Africa is an example. But liberation theology developed in other parts of Africa as a reaction to injustice and oppression.

Liberation theologians have helped the church by reminding us of issues of justice. But liberation hermeneutics often imposes its own presuppositions on a text. Then the text is made to conform to one's liberation presuppositions. Then one wonders again whether we are hearing the word of God or the word of man.

---

[30]G. Osborne, *The Hermeneutical Spiral*, p. 478.
[31]See G. Osborne, *The Hermeneutical Spiral*, pp. 482-83.

Feminist hermeneutics is a form of liberation hermeneutics. Feminists will examine the text of Scripture to see if the text is biased in the favor of women or against women. They even identify "texts of terror" in the Bible.

> Feminist exegetes approach the text without pretense about some undefinable objectivity. Feminists are quite willing to acknowledge that they are reading the text through the lens of feminism.[32]

In Africa and elsewhere there is a growing interest in the readers' response to a text. Justin Ukpong has developed an *inculturation hermeneutics*. He feels that a text can best be interpreted in the context of a local indigenous community.

Such an approach is interesting. But unfortunately Ukpong ends up with a postmodern view of truth. He says:

> the meaning of a text is a function of the interaction between the text in its context and the reader in his/her context. Thus, there is no one absolute meaning of a text to be recovered through historical analysis alone.[33]

But it is our belief that an exegete should first of all seek the original intended meaning of a text; after that the relevance of such a text could be explored in such reading communities.

But not all global theology is postmodern. The significant *Africa Bible Commentary* is a prime example of evangelical Africans searching for the original meaning of the text of Scripture and applying it to the local context.

---

[32] Hayes and Holladay, *Biblical Exegesis*, p. 170.

[33] J. Ukpong, "Developments in Biblical Interpretation in Africa: Historical and Hermeneutical Directions," in *The Bible in Africa* (Leiden: Brill, 2000), p. 24.

Conclusion

Scripture is God's Word for his church. For two thousand years the church has listened to God's Word in Scripture. Scripture has been enormously formative for the life of the church.

Hermeneutics and exegesis are important for understanding and hearing God's Word in Scripture. The history of exegesis gives us positive and negative examples of how to interpret Scripture. In the end, a good exegetical methodology will examine the text of Scripture to allow God to speak clearly to our lives.

Study Questions

1. What was Jesus' view of the Old Testament?
2. How did the second-century church respond to the Gnostic and Marcionist heresies?
3. What are the different exegetical methods of the schools of Alexandria and Antioch?
4. What is the problem of a four-fold interpretation of Scripture?
5. What was Martin Luther's answer to the four-fold interpretation of Scripture?
6. What is the problem with rationalism?
7. What is the postmodern view of truth?
8. What is an evangelical response to postmodernism?

SAMPLE THESIS OUTLINES

The Tower of Babel
An Exegetical Study of Genesis 11:1-9

Chapter One: Introduction
   1.1 Background to study
   1.2 Statement of problem
   1.3 Statement of purpose
   1.4 Methodology
   1.5 Literature review

Chapter Two: Literary Context of the Text
   2.1 Book context: structure of Genesis
   2.2 Immediate context: the genealogies
   2.3 Genre of the text

Chapter Three: Structure and Notes on the Text
   3.1 Verses 1-2: The setting
   3.2 Verses 3-4: The rebellion
   3.3 Verses 5-7: God's response
   3.4 Verses 8-9: The result

Chapter Four: Relevance of the text
   4.1 Pride in our society

4.2 Languages in our society

Chapter Five: Conclusion and Recommendations
5.1 Conclusion
5.2 Recommendations

Salvation in the Psalms
An Exegetical Study of Psalm 3

Chapter One: Introduction

1.1 Background to study

1.2 Statement of problem

1.3 Statement of purpose

1.4 Methodology

Chapter Two: Literature Review of Salvation in Psalm 3

2.1 Commentaries teaching salvation as spiritual salvation

2.2 Commentaries teaching salvation as physical salvation

2.3 Commentaries teaching salvation as wholistic salvation

Chapter Three: Word Study

3.1 Yasha (to save)

3.2 Yeshua (salvation)

Chapter Four: Exegesis of Psalm 3

4.1 Hebrew text

4.2 English translation

4.3 Structure of text

4.3.1 Verses 1-2: lament

4.3.2 Verses 3-4: petition

4.3.3 Verses 5-6: trust

4.3.4 Verses 7-8: petition and trust

4.4 Salvation in Psalm 3

Chapter Five: Conclusion and Relevance

5.1 Conclusion

5.2 Relevance to the African situation

An Exegetical Study of Amos 5:14-15

Chapter One: Introduction
1.1 Background to study
1.2 Statement of problem
1.3 Statement of purpose
1.4 Methodology
1.5 Literature review

Chapter Two: Context of Amos 5:14-15
2.1 Historical context
2.2 Literary context

Chapter Three: Word Study
3.1 Tov (good)
3.2 Ra (evil)
3.3 Hanan (gracious)

Chapter Four: Exegesis of Amos 5:14-15
4.1 Hebrew text
4.2 English translation
4.3 Genre of the text
4.4 Structure of the text
4.5 Meaning of the text

Chapter Five: Conclusion and Relevance
5.1 Conclusion
5.2 Relevance to the Nigerian situation

Baptism with the Holy Spirit and Fire
An Exegetical Study of Luke 3:15-18

Chapter One: Introduction

    1.1 Background to study

    1.2 Statement of problem

    1.3 Statement of purpose

    1.4 Methodology

    1.5 Definition of terms

Chapter Two: Literature Review

    2.1 Baptism with fire as a Pentecostal blessing

    2.2 Baptism with fire as judgment

Chapter Three: Word Study

    3.1 *Baptizo* in Luke

    3.2 *Baptizo* in the New Testament

Chapter Four: Exegesis of Text

    4.1 Greek text

    4.2 English translation

    4.3 Notes on the text

    4.4 Meaning of the text

Chapter Five: Summary and Recommendations

    5.1 Summary

    5.2 Recommendations

The Millennium
An Exegetical Study of Revelation 20:1-15

Chapter One: Introduction
1.1 Background to study
1.2 Statement of problem
1.3 Statement of purpose
1.4 Methodology

Chapter Two: Literature Review
2.1 The millennium as a literal thousand years
2.2 The millennium as a figurative period of time

Chapter Three: Historical and Literary Context
3.1 Historical background
3.2 Literary background: structure of Revelation
3.3 Genre of Revelation

Chapter Four: Exegesis of text
4.1 Greek text
4.2 English translation
4.3 Structure of text
4.3.1 Verses 1-3: Binding of Satan
4.3.2 Verses 4-6: Reign of Christ
4.3.3 Verses 7-9: The Last Battle
4.3.4 Verses 10-15: The Last Judgment
4.4 Meaning of the Text

Chapter Five: Summary and Recommendations
5.1 Summary
5.2 Recommendations

BIBLIOGRAPHY

Africa Bible Commentary. Edited by T. Adeyamo et al. Nairobi: Word Alive, 2006.

Aland, Kurt and Barbara Aland. *The Text of the New Testament*. Revised edition. Translated by E. Rhodes. Grand Rapids: Eerdmans, 1989.

Alter, Robert. *The Art of Biblical Narrative*. Revised edition. New York: Basic Books, 2011.

Biblia Hebraica Stuttgartensia. Edited by K. Elliger *et al*. Stuttgart: Deutsche Bibelgesellschaft, 1990.

Boer, Harry. *A Short History of the Early Church*. Ibadan: Daystar Press, 1976.

Bright, John. *The Authority of the Old Testament*. Nashville: Abingdon, 1967; reprint ed., Carlisle: Paternoster Press, 1997.

Brotzman, Ellis. *Old Testament Textual Criticism*. Grand Rapids: Baker, 1994.

Calvin, John. *Galatians, Ephesians, Philippians and Colossians*. (Calvin's New Testament Commentaries). Translated by T.H.L. Parker. Grand Rapids: Eerdmans, 1965.

Collins, John J. *The Bible after Babel: Historical Criticism in a Postmodern Age*. (Calvin's New Testament Commentaries). Translated by T.H.L. Parker. Grand Rapids: Eerdmans, 2005.

Deppe, Dean. *All Roads Lead to the Text*. Grand Rapids: Eerdmans, 2011.

Egger, Wilhelm. *How To Read the New Testament*. Translated by P. Heinegg. Edited and introduction by Hendrikus Boers. Peabody, Mass.: Hendrickson, 1996.

Fee, Gordon. *New Testament Exegesis*. 3rd edition. Louisville: Westminster John Knox, 2002.

Fee, Gordon and Douglas Stuart. *How To Read the Bible for All Its Worth*. Grand Rapids: Zondervan, 1982; reprint ed., Jos: Potters House, 1999.

Gorman, Michael. *Elements of Biblical Exegesis.* Revised edition. Peabody, Mass.: Hendrickson, 2009.

Grant, Robert and David Tracy. *A Short History os the Interpretation of the Bible.* Revised edition. Minneapolis: Fortress, 1984.

Hayes, John and Carl Holladay. *Biblical Exegesis.* 3rd edition. Louisville: Westminster John Knox, 2007.

Hendriksen, William. *More Than Conquerors.* Grand Rapids: Baker, 1939.

Kaiser, Walter and Moisés Silva. *Introduction to Biblical Hermeneutics.* Revised edition. Grand Rapids: Zondervan, 2007.

Klein, William, Craig Blomberg and Robert Hubbard. *Introduction to Biblical Interpretation.* Revised edition. Nashville: Thomas Nelson, 2004.

Longenecker, Richard. *Biblical Exegesis in the Apostolic Period.* Revised edition. Grand Rapids: Eerdmans, 1999.

Luther, Martin. "Answer to . . . Emser," in *Luther's Works,* 39:137-224. Philadelphia: Fortress Press, 1970.

Luther, Martin. *Table Talk.* (Luther's Works, vol. 54.). Philadelphia: Fortress Press, 1967.

Luther, Martin. "The Babylonian Captivity of the Church," in *Luther's Works,* 36:4-126. Philadelphia: Muhlenberg Press, 1959.

Nichols, Stephen. *Martin Luther.* Phillipsburg, NJ: P&R, 2002.

Osborne, Grant. *The Hermeneutical Spiral.* Revised edition. Downers Grove: InterVarsity Press, 2006.

Palmer, Timothy. *A Theology of the New Testament.* Bukuru: Africa Christian Textbooks, 2012.

Palmer, Timothy. *A Theology of the Old Testament.* Bukuru: Africa Christian Textbooks, 2011.

Palmer, Timothy. *Theological Research Methods.* Bukuru: Africa Christian Textbooks, 2012.

Preus, Jonathan. *Reading the Bible through Christ.* Bukuru: Africa Christian Textbooks, 1997.

Preuss, Horst D. *Old Testament Theology.* 2 volumes. Translated by L. Perdue. Louisville: Westminster John Knox, 1995, 1996.

Return to Babel: Global Perspectives on the Bible. Edited by J. Levison and P. Pope-Levison. Louisville: Westminster John Knox, 1999.

Stuart, Douglas. *Old Testament Exegesis.* 4th edition. Louisville: Westminster John Knox, 2009.

The Greek New Testament. Edited by K. Aland *et al.* New York: United Bible Societies, 1966.

Ukpong, Justin. "Developments in Biblical Interpretation in Africa: Historical and Hermeneutical Directions." In *The Bible in Africa*, pp. 11-28. Edited by G. West and M. Dube. Leiden: Brill, 2000.

Ukpong, Justin. "Inculturation Hermeneutics: An African Approach to Biblical Interpretation." In *The Bible in a World Context*, pp. 17-32. Edited by W. Dietrich and U. Luz. Grand Rapids: Eerdmans, 2002.